HOW THE WATER HOLDS ME

HOW THE WATER HOLDS ME

POEMS

TARIQ LUTHUN

BULL★CITY
PRESS
DURHAM, NC

How the Water Holds Me

Editors' Selection from the 2019 Frost Place Chapbook Competition

Library of Congress Cataloging-in-Publication Data
Luthun, Tariq
How the Water Holds Me: poems / by Tariq Luthun
p. cm.

ISBN-13: 978-1-949344-13-4

Published in the United States of America

S P O C K

Book design by Spock and Associates

Cover artwork by Majdoleen Faraj
www.instagram.com/majdoleeen_96

Published by
BULL CITY PRESS
1217 Odyssey Drive
Durham, NC 27713
www.BullCityPress.com

CONTENTS

HOW THE WATER HOLDS ME

THE SUMMER MY COUSIN WENT MISSING

I should have asked how our khalto was holding
up, but I knew where she would be: her body

weary & unkind, buried in the day's tasks; back turned
to the home she grew up in; seeds in the

farm's soil, like miracles, sprouting as
she tends to them. Is this not always the case?

Child upon child goes, and someone's mother
is no longer a mother. My aunt — a mother herself — looks,

for a moment, away; nothing she plants has roots
long enough to hold. She turns back anyway, looks

ahead. If we are too caught up in the end — like boys
fleeing from the day's news — eyes worried

about that which we cannot control,
how ever will we stay fed? How ever

will we live long enough to grieve?

FRUIT

as kin rise to pray in the deepest shade
before each dawn, i ask: what is it about
      a seed shedding itself into
      a seed reborn that makes it
its name? still i wait, as though there is
      no time for question through the
      tired feast we become in this
moonlight before the fast. mama speaks:

كُلْ كُلْ يَالَّا خُذْ خُذْ

eat, eat. go on. take, take.
      and i take
      after my father
who used to pull crabapples
      ripe off the trees
      lining this morbid
crackle of roads

that will never belong
to us. as my mother runs
      her wet fingertips into dates
      beneath the rinse, my father would
say: *americans are*
      too busy watching good fruit
      wither away.
too busy wrapping their teeth around

the skin of other things
in the evening hours. meanwhile,
      we just gnaw through that. he and i
      take all of our time —

it is the only thing our families ask of us.
           and, again, i ask:
           what makes a brown boy his
name? when does he become

a feast of *yes*,
a game of *eat, eat. take, take.* a riddle:
           what color of boy doesn't eat
           what his mother makes him?
what being could leap
           out of a seed and walk
           upright just long enough
to inhale the dirt that will see him

a man? here, we get tired of this
script, muddled
           film of hardened juice, and thickened
           erasure; the shedding of
flesh into soil. *O how much*
           easier can we be to take?
           another generation passes
into the wake, and mama prays in the moonlight

before the fast. this is where i come
to learn why a mother gives
           her kin a name that lingers, a name
           that only we can pronounce.

PEOPLE, DRUNK AT PARTIES, TELL ME THEY LOVE ME

My mother — who does not go to parties, and has never touched
alcohol — tells me the same thing: *I love you*. I don't know

why it's so difficult for me to say, let alone believe it. I'd like to
blame my father, but it doesn't seem fair to that man, one who comes

from a realm of rubied sand and air thick enough to hold
upon undrenching forehead into palm. I've seen the land, trust

me. I would take you if I could, but I haven't —
in over a decade — been allowed to return. Taking my parents'

lead, it was the first love I knew. Each time I went back,
I would open wide to fill my arms with the sun, and my mouth

would take in everything below the sky until I became my cousins.
For years, this language was the only tongue I cared for.

Yet this doesn't seem to explain it: that all I was
was a boy who once loved a place that is no longer his.

Love, I have learned to be not something

received, but something given. So many
hold it like a glass after their bellies have

seized from it the liquor. I've done enough
damage to myself to run me into the bottle's

arms, and this is where I wonder what leads
so many to end the day drinking. Are they like me,

yearning yet unable to return to that which fed them?
This might just be how some of us choose

to cope: call for everything
we wish to receive, then hope

we are delivered something
sober; something fully present

and unafraid of where it hasn't been.

WE ALREADY KNOW THIS

There is more to us than
what was taken from us.

A place to call
home. Land of olive trees,
and their branches.
Palestine. There,
I've said it. I want to be sure
everyone knows where my parents
hail from. Each of us
needs a place to return to. Genocide:
I would hope everyone knows
did not start, and did not end
at the Holocaust. I haven't forgotten that
everyone needs a place on this planet. And I,
I prefer to live where I can leave
the doors unlocked —
or live without the doors —
or hell. I don't even care
for walls. But, I do care
for the blues: water, the sadness
that comes when it is not within
sight. I don't know if there is
a child, anywhere on this earth, that wasn't,
at least once, held by their mother. Water:
where my mother held me
until I was given to land. O firm land —
how my father holds me — people keep calling
for blood, to dress you in it.
I don't think any of them

know, truly, how much of it
the body can take; how much
the body can lose.

HARB

When piqued, boys be a bone.
Be a tantrum, a cracked tomb

of discipline exorcising itself
into the backs of boys they had

no business putting our fists
inside of. I tried so hard

to find myself in the spines of the men
who wronged me. As told by

my mother: all good is holy, while evil
finds itself in those

                    who do not sleep, those
                    who lie

awake learning to write and
heed, and pray; in me,

this wired thing. My father did all he could
to be sure I was birthed with a beating

fist to go with those sleepless beasts,
my lungs. We find — to this day — a book

of versed calligraphy is the prettiest
flesh to make a lamb of.
This is what I will tell my son
when he is beckoned by

the bully in him; if his scorn loses
sight of its prey. If my son develops
a taste for blood,
I will blame it on

my father's enemies, and
our ancestors. One day, he will ask me about the red
                in the river
                of our name,

where it turned.
When he does, I will
have the same answer I did
when my parents told me to hold
                my tongue and cleanse
                my fistful

heart: *I do not know what to throw away
when nothing belongs to me.*

SEED

Always ready
        to give,
the men in my family know
anger like an open palm.

Last week, brother threw
a punch, & i decided
not to break him. Last night,
baba went in on
me: my lack of
        a job.
        a wife.
        a god.
i love
to tell him they are one
and the same. When i meet my mother,
i talk to her like a man
talks to himself: full
        of inherited simmer,
        slow & wayward
as we both wait for
        our blood to dry,
        our fathers to call us home

ODE TO BROWN CHILD ON AN AIRPLANE FOR THE FIRST TIME

I don't remember if I, too, was afraid,
but I do remember when the sky was
our thing — I could say the word: *flight*

and, in its stead, none would hear *fight*
spill from my jaw. The last time it took
a punch, I was in the boy's bathroom,

surrounded — by boys — as a boy
unleashed his fist into me. I returned
the favor into his gut, and ran. Moments

before, he had called me *gay*, but I wasn't
sure why I had to defend my glee — scarce
as it was. Hours later, a mess of tears

ran through me as I was pulled from gym
by the principal and suspended for defending
what little parts of myself I could still call

mine. I don't know why *this* is the story
I choose to tell, but I do know that I may
forget it once we take off; shedding the skin

that everyone fears of releasing
toward the sun. Beautiful,
isn't it, to be able to leave behind

this world, its lost and angry boys.

I SING THIS ELEGY FOR THE NAMELESS

moon I watch in the morning before my old man wakes up
to call me on all the wrong I've done. When I used to pray,
I saw myself a dove: sun through my wings,

God lifting my back into the gunmetal-grey sky.
When I stopped calling out
to deities, some might have seen me

a crow: God beneath me and my
belly, as I cried and cried out
for anyone to take me from

my solitude; yet no body knows
the truth. In these hours meant
for slumber, I wager that not all

creatures with wings know flight; and
there is no time for rest when
even the snakes lay eggs.

The sky is too heavy now, and what good
is the earth if the fallen is all we find
there? Those old men buried

all in the dark
with their shovels, and
called us the sin.

PORTRAIT OF MY FATHER DROWNING

in the type of love he deserves; nestled
in his lap, a young me is learning
how to swim. I flounder in
water that is only knee deep,

while, fully dressed on the pool's
edge, my mother records
the lesson. *Blood will always*
be outweighed by the body

of water it wades into. Earth,
itself, I realize, is just a body
of waters. Years later, I spend a summer
patrolling a different pool's edge. I lose

count of how many sons are held
by their fathers; large &
calloused hands buoying
their lineages, these islands

and their fluttering limbs.

I JUST WANT EVERYONE TO UNDERSTAND

that I spent a good portion of
my youth alongside my sister — we played

computer games; often, a bootleg version
of Sailor Moon. Sometimes, I cry

at the thought of how we used to be
close. That isn't the case today, but

what can I expect after having
done what I did: channeling

the pain others have caused me. I once heard
a scripture: *no weapon wielded against you shall*

prosper; I imagine the weapon being spoken of
is me. I became familiar with eating

alone, poised, in high school, atop
porcelain at lunchtime. I never called

anyone *mine*, except for those who made a habit
of bullying me — *my* bullies. I can't blame them,

though — we rarely know what
we are, much less what we are

doing to one another — especially as
children. I grew up, and realized

the only language I'd ever been comfortable
speaking is one usually wielded against people —

English. I'm not surprised. Nobody can hate that
which shares their tongue, they say. I fear what becomes

of the family that feasts on pain, if it perseveres or grows
accustomed to the ache of assimilation. When I stop

to consider my unyielding desire to have everyone
like me, I think: *start with the mouth*.

UPON LEAVING THE DIAMOND TO CATCH 14
STITCHES IN MY BROW

You and I will never be more
brothers than we were
in the heat that summer,

in the park, when the bat,
newly painted in my blood,
lit my father to yell

at all the other kids playing baseball who
know, now, the sound of men
— darker — from a different world: hurt, ready,

and loud. Our fathers — and the off-white
noise they let loose — didn't help,
and might have

made matters worse. I wake up
in the back of an all-white room
I do not recognize, its luminescence

bouncing off the walls. I come
to know this room — place I had
never been — while you continue running

circles around the neighbors, lest their
tongues point toward our families' names;
lest they — for the first time — see us

bleed and think: *prey*.

FINDING MYSELF IN THE DIRECT MESSAGES OF SOMEONE I DO NOT KNOW IS IN KUWAIT

There is something to be said of
culture; how I end up here: the simplest

explanation might be that my father won't stop
making jokes about how he can't wait until

I get married so that he can be done
with me. Perhaps — unknown to her —

it is my mother's doing: her aging
pride would like grandchildren. Maybe

it is our elders, that they seek a youth
that their bodies can no longer

possess. Or maybe, our bodies seek
to possess a youth that keeps us

from becoming our elders. Each evening
erupts a fight between my family

and me, arguing about where my life is
headed, battling over the places my body

lands. I haven't settled down
with a woman — I'm not sure

I'd like to. And yet, here
I go, drenched in desire that isn't

entirely mine. I've left so many
times — and so much — to find

what might come of flinging
oneself into thirst; to drown

in every possibility, and
learn — if it's possible —

to emerge unscathed
from its mouth.

I WONDER ABOUT THE WOMAN WHO NOW LIVES IN THE BALAD WITHOUT ME

She said: *again*. My palms
open, and I wonder
about control — who

it belongs to. A woman
I loved once begged me
to choke her, and I did. I did

this after I made
sure she could handle
the prospect of me

wrapping my fingers
around her neck — small
wrenches digging into

her collar until all she had left
was silence, my grip
easing to slowly

let oxygen back
into her lungs. Muted
fiends, my hands —

we simply don't let go
of the tools that coax
what we crave into being.

Again — it's not enough. Somewhere, in the lot
of a suburban hotel, all that is left

is us begging, begging

to keep away.

POLITICAL POEM

Blessed be the Transportation Security Administration
agent for, after flagging my red duffel bag at the airport, allowing
me — who, in the winter months, is a rather light-skinned Arab-
American — upon several minutes of careful debate,
to keep my organic coconut oil so that I — despite having
bought the container from a certain Midwest superstore's
baking section — might apply this essential moisturizer to my thirsty
skin, because it is quite abundantly clear that the contained substance is
safe: solid at room temperature, and — when in its purest form — white.

I FELT NOTHING

when I, again, rode

the rollercoaster at

a certain American theme park,

hoping that it would bring me

some joy; the thrill that comes

with being shot through air

I'd never, otherwise, experience.

Yet, not a single feeling passed

through me, save for the discontent

that comes with knowing that

no matter how little time it takes

for me to turn point A into point B, I will

never become wind — I will always be

a skeleton marked by the flesh that holds it;

attire that can get me through a turnstile,

but not necessarily a checkpoint

at the airport or the other airport or

a border. *Do you see it?* How lovely

it would be to become something

that cannot be contained; to become

something so present, yet so far out

of reach that no man even thinks of trying

to lay his hands on it.

AFTER SPENDING AN EVENING IN NOVEMBER TRYING TO CONVINCE MY MOTHER THAT WE'LL BE FINE

I imagine it isn't easy to accept
that the coverage of

the world outside can be spun

so much; that in just one night,
so much of what we thought we

knew can vanish, despite us
having seen all the deaths

from down the street unfold
on TV. It was "great

for ratings," and this is why
I reason that humans are just terrible

inventors — much better as
innovators. Most can't think

of new ways to persist, so they run
with whatever messaging makes the most

noise, hoping the sound spins
into a tune enough people can sing

& dance to. Yet, all
my peoples and I still ask

if it's possible for a man,
immigrant as my father —

without having moved
an inch — to one day

awaken from the dream
and enter — upon leaving

a country that cannot have him —
a country that does not want him.

AL-BAĦR

I have seen death
look like me: bones sprawled
out somewhere between

hazel-coded grains along
the beach of the Red
Sea's shore — a palm opened and

a palm closed — body thick as
a fist in waning crimson tides.
Still, I've never known
a law to rewind a bullet

or a bomb, to unwind
a spine too busy wrapped
around Grief. I am told

we must learn to speak
with its tongue: too mired
in the end. I have seen this
all before: I watch men

who don't (and sometimes do) look like me
print tomorrow's face with my mothers'
graves. I'm incoherent

at this point, but I saw
a boy that could have become
me wash up on a shore.
Along another, I watched all

the boys lose a match. I guess
I'm not putting enough blame
on the child.

       Don't get me
wrong. I'm just
wondering: can a boy
       find death, and not

       bring it home
to show everyone
what he's found?

FOR THOSE WE LEFT BEHIND

each day i ask my mother
what we do
                 when we can't fight,
                 and there is no money
left to give. tired, she raises
                 her eyes from the dishes,
                 her hands up from the bath,
and gives
                 a gentle laugh,
                 a sigh, *we make*
                 du'a, we pray

                 for whatever remains
           after the sea rises
to swallow our shore

SERMON (FOR THOSE WHO SURVIVE)

If every day above ground is blessed,
then when will we sip a wine that does not flow

from the wounds hallowing our bellies? Where does this
vineyard lie, the one where our blood remains

just that? Every day, I crawl out of this cage,
elbows crimsoned & so fine; so aged with the sky's

knees in my back. My cries flutter & my throat loosens
to make space like a prison emptying its cells

into the earth below the earth. Now, here, I am
miles away & leagues above, watching

my cousins in the Holy Land drown in someone else's comfort;
another's desire for luxury. Cursed, I watch

the lexicon grow & grow. & god, I find
in every throne I lust;
      I shook
god in every breath I'd
hush. & whispered:

I'm king
      so long as I'm able /
I'm good
      so long as I'm feared /
I'm full
      so long as I'm stable /

I'm prey

    so long as I'm here.

I CHOSE NOT TO

after Lucille Clifton

get help. I've arrived
at a man draping himself

in the wardrobe of
the dead. I watched this

scene become my life
the way a hatchling leaves

a nest: young until
youth is shed

by the hunger
for a calm

belly. How many
children, never to

return, flutter into
the offing? I wake

        up. And I pray
        for everything
that has not tried
to kill me; feeling
        blessed, I pray
        for everything

that has tried
      and failed. I pray
      for everything:

a body that has, as a weapon,
only wielded hands; a body

that has only ever failed
to claim a life, including
      its own.

POEM IN WHICH SLEEP IS NOT A METAPHOR

for Death.
Or a cousin of it;
not a premonition,
or a close friend.
Death has no family,
it's fine on its own;
ceaseless, its ability to seize
my body's comfort. I'd love
to say that I'm fine with everything
ending at this very moment.
But, what will my mother think
if all I am to become is an empty
room, unworn shoes, poems
on a hard drive, leftovers
growing old in a fridge
at work until someone
decides its time
to throw it all
away?

I GO TO THE BACKYARD TO PICK MINT LEAVES FOR MY MOTHER

Today, my mouth fell
wide when I saw the light
slip into the hills, and those boys

I grew up with did not
come back. Or, so I hear. Mama
would often ask me to gather

the mint leaves from behind our home,
and so I would leave for this
nectar — without it, there is nothing sweet

to speak of. I pray that
when I am gone, my people speak
as sweetly of me as I do of them.

I see us, often, steeped
in the land and hope that
a shore remains

a shore — not a place to become
yesterday. The girls have joined the boys
now — all of them

tucked just beyond
the earth. But I know they wouldn't run
from their mothers — not without a fight,

a chase, a hunt, a honey, a home

for the tea to settle; a haven
for us to return to.

ACKNOWLEDGMENTS

Versions of these poems first appeared in the following journals:

Crab Orchard Review: "Portrait of My Father Drowning"
Drunk in a Midnight Choir: "Al-Bahr" and "Sermon"
Literary Hub: "We Already Know This"
Michigan Quarterly Review: "I Felt Nothing" and "The Summer My Cousin Went Missing"
Mizna: "Upon Leaving the Diamond to Catch 14 Stitches in My Brow"
Sidekick Lit: "For Those We Left Behind"
Up the Staircase Quarterly: "Fruit"
Vinyl Poetry: "Seed"
Wildness: "Harb"

First and forever, I give thanks to my family — my parents, and my siblings — who have always been there, offering a home for me to return to each day. My aunts and uncles, whose love stops for no border. My ever-growing collection of cousins whose desire to remain connected in the face of all obstacles continues to astound me. I am grateful to our ancestors for setting all of us into motion, and the Higher Power that lets us be.

I am grateful to the lands I call home — from Detroit to North Carolina to Palestine, and beyond — for gifting me with Swati Rayasam, Sonia Ali, Inam Kang, Alexandra Wee, the Sabris, Luther Hughes, Lauren Bullock, Jon Jon Moore, Diannely Antigua, Roy Guzman, Kamelya Youssef, Isra El-beshir, Phillip B. Williams, Sue Welker, C. Dale Young, Martha Rhodes, Gabrielle Calvocoressi, Dasan Ahanu, Baba Darryl E. Jordan, Andrew Malcolm Dooley, Gabriel Ramirez, Chanda Prescod-Weinstein, Zahraa Nasser, Jeremy Allen, Matthew Stiffler, Maya Younis, Matthew Wrase, William Evans, William Nu'utupu Giles, Mahogany L. Browne, Mimi Wong, Melissa Tolentino, John Buckley, Jess Rizkallah, Carlos Andrés

Gómez, Leah Nieboer, Sarah Soliman, Edwin Bodney, Zachary Caballero, George Abraham, Marwa Helal, Raphael Mina Eissa, Victor Jackson, Rasha Anayah, LaShaun Phoenix Kotaran, Whitney Syphax Walker, Afaq Mahmoud, Dalia Altarshan, Bernard Ferguson, Justin Rogers, Brittany Rogers, Tarfia Faizullah, Sumaiya Zama, Nadine Marshall, Tiana Nobile, Lily Chiu-Watson, Jinan Safko, Sterling Higa, Robalu Gibson, Amin Dallal, Remi Kanazi, Remi Kanazi, Tawana Petty, Lena Khalaf Tuffaha, Marlin M. Jenkins, Jamaal May, Hanif Abdurraqib, Aaron Samuels, Cynthia Franklin, Asil Yassine, Garret Potter, Lindsay Stone, Michael Rosen, Sam Cook, Dylan Garity, Marlena Moore, Carlina Duan, Ken Norman, Joe Kantor, Susan M. Darraj, Hannah Matsunaga, Matthew Olzmann, RJ Walker, Nisa Dang, Shannon Garcia, Will McInerney, Jive Poetic, Roya Marsh, Paul Tran, Ari Brown, Hannah Torres Peet, Alan Shapiro, Kristian Davis Bailey, Deonte Osayande, Dana Dajani, Shannon Matesky, Danez Smith, Safia Elhillo, Dior Gabrielle, Christin Lee, Scott Woods, Jon Curtis, Ashia Ajani, Chinaka Hodge, Crystal Nance, Autumn Atchley, Matthew Taylor, Sonya Larson, Lyz Soto, Freddie M. Clark, Michael Highland, DJ Rogers, Suja Sawafta, Amal Kassir, Mohammed Safi, Fatima Abbas, and so many others who have held me at various points in my life and labor, whether through the kindness they've offered or the adoration I have for their work.

I am blessed to have been welcomed into spaces like the Cass Corridor Commons, the Arab American National Museum, *The Offing*, the Program for Writers at Warren Wilson College, too many masajid and Muslim communities to list, Sacrificial Poets and the Jambalaya Soul Slam, Brave New Voices and its Future Corps, UM Slam, the Detroit and Ann Arbor poetry communities, the Neutral Zone, InsideOut Literary Arts, the Rustbelt Poetry Festival, Button Poetry, the Radius of Arab American Writers, Inc. (RAWI), the Palestinian Youth Movement, the greater organizing community of Palestinians and our allies, Jewish Voice for Peace, The Collective for Disability Justice in Detroit, The Watering Hole, Bull City Press, and so many other communities in which I have cultivated my praxis and sense of purpose. You have offered me so many chosen kin that I am physically unable to thank them all here.

ABOUT THE AUTHOR

TARIQ LUTHUN is a data consultant, community organizer, and poet from Detroit, MI. He earned his MFA in Poetry from the Program for Writers at Warren Wilson College and serves as Editor of the Micro Department at *The Offing*. Luthun's writing has earned him an Emmy Award and the honor of *Best of the Net*. His work has appeared in *Vinyl Poetry*, *Lit Hub*, *Mizna*, *Winter Tangerine Review*, and *Button Poetry*, among others. The son of Palestinian immigrants, Luthun is committed to the liberation of all marginalized peoples and works to ensure we can all return home.